Punctuation

KINGFISHER
NEW YORK

KINGFISHER
LONDON & NEW YORK

Copyright © Kingfisher 2010
Book concept copyright © Toucan 2010
Illustration copyright © Simon Basher 2010

Published in the United States by Kingfisher,
175 Fifth Ave., New York, NY 10010
Kingfisher is an imprint of Macmillan Children's Books, London.
All rights reserved.

Consultant: Orin K. Hargraves

Designed and created by Basher
www.basherbooks.com
www.basherworld.com
www.bebo.com/simonbasher

Dedicated to Sandra Coleman

Distributed in the U.S. by Macmillan, 175 Fifth Ave., New York, NY 10010
Distributed in Canada by H.B. Fenn and Company Ltd.,
34 Nixon Road, Bolton, Ontario L7E 1W2

Library of Congress Cataloging-in-Publication data has been applied for.

ISBN: 978-0-7534-6420-5

Kingfisher books are available for special promotions and premiums.
For details contact: Special Markets Department, Macmillan,
175 Fifth Avenue, New York, NY 10010.

For more information, please visit www.kingfisherbooks.com

Printed in Taiwan
9 8 7 6 5 4 3 2 1
1TR/1209/SHENS/UNT/126.6MA/C

Note to readers: The website addresses listed above are correct at the time of going to print. However, due to the ever-changing nature of the Internet, website addresses and content can change. Websites can contain links that are unsuitable for children. The publisher cannot be held responsible for changes in website addresses or content or for information obtained through a third party. We strongly advise that Internet searches are supervised by an adult.

CONTENTS

Sentence

* A gaggle of words that makes complete sense on its own
* Sturdy character who is formed with a subject and a predicate
* Punctuation marks line up and clip on to its outstretched arms

I am a determined character who stands on my own two feet. I always have a purpose. I can tell you something: *The cat was fed.* Ask a question: *Have you fed the cat?* Give an order: *Please feed the cat!* Or express a feeling: *What a beautiful cat!*

I have two parts. Let's take, *The cat was sick.* The person or thing I talk about is called the subject—"The cat." Enough of that cat! And what I say or write about the subject is called the predicate—"was sick." See, it takes two! You get my point. I'm basic. Words on their own are fine, but I'm the one who gathers them together so they say something. That's my purpose! To help make me clear and easy to read, you need to meet some marks— the punctuation team.

✓ **DO** start a sentence with a capital letter and finish it with a period, a question mark, or an exclamation point: *The pirates boarded the ship and stole the treasure.*

✓ **DO** be sure that a sentence makes complete sense on its own. This makes sense on its own: *The pirates boarded the ship.* This does not: *stole the treasure.*

Sentence

Capital Letters

☀ Big letters that stand tall, like this: A, B, C, D, E . . . Z
☀ One of the basics of writing—they are used to start sentences
☀ Small shrinking-violet lowercase letters are their little brothers

We are the top dogs, the head honchos, the whole enchilada. You don't get higher or mightier than the first letter in the first word of every Sentence, do you? When one of us shows up at the front of a word, the word stands for something special—one of a kind. Our "B" is the difference between your friend Bill—he is one of a kind, all right—and the bill you get from the plumber.

We give the word "I" its "I-ness." It stands tall and capital, even when it is used in the middle of a sentence. Words that use us get respect, whether they are place names (Spain, New York, Mount Everest), nationalities (Mexican, Chinese), or dates (Monday, July 14). And in case you think we take ourselves too seriously, let us tell you that we are up for fun and feasting, too: Thanksgiving, Kwanzaa.

✓ **DO** use a capital letter at the start of a sentence, as well as for people's names, place names, nationalities, languages, days of the week, and months. Also use capital letters for "I" and titles (*Mr., Mrs., Dr.*).

✗ **DON'T** use capital letters for the seasons: *spring, summer, fall, winter*.

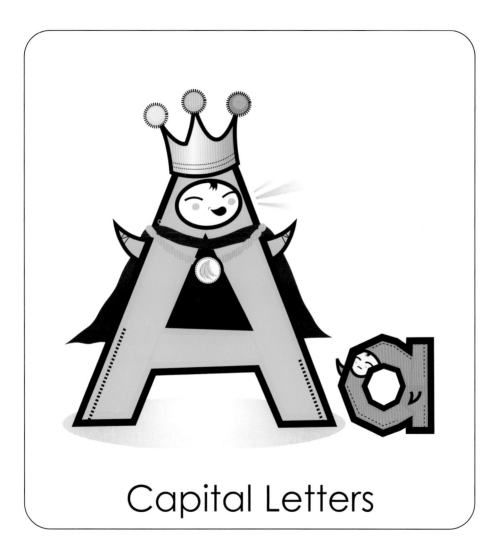

Capital Letters

Chapter 1
The Basic Bunch

Period, Question Mark, and Exclamation Point—this handy threesome hold it all together. They are key items in your punctuation toolbox, like nails or screws. The Basic Bunch members are small, and it's easy to miss them, but don't be fooled. Hammered in at the ends of sentences, they're vital, the basics. You can't do without them. How do you know when to use them? Now that you've met all three, read on and find out! Learn the tricks of their trade and you can be sure that anything you write will be sturdy and do what it's supposed to do—like a well-made table or chair.

Period

Question Mark

Exclamation Point

. **Period**

▥ The Basic Bunch

✳ A punchy little statement stopper
✳ Small but perfectly formed, this dot is king of the Basic Bunch
✳ It can be used when words are shortened, as in *U.S.A.*

Small, round, and forceful—that's me. I'm the limit. I'm the end. The statement has been made. The Sentence is over. Time's up, and I'm the fella who gets up to say, "That's all, folks." When you've made up your mind and know what you want to say, there I stand in basic black, ready to give your thoughts the finish they need.

You can't write for long without me. I stand between one statement and the next. If I weren't around, people wouldn't know where on earth they are. Where's the end? What's the beginning? Yikes! What a mess! By the way, Question Mark and Exclamation Point sometimes stand in for me. Okay, they're fun for a while, but when your punctuation partying is over, you'll come right back to me—cool, calm, collected, and very much to the point.

✓ **DO** use a period at the end of a sentence with a normal amount of emphasis. It can also be used at the end of an abbreviation, such as *Dr.* (abbreviation of "Doctor.")

✗ **DON'T** use a period at the end of a sentence that asks a question or shows strong feeling, such as surprise, shock, or anger.

Period

? **Question Mark**

The Basic Bunch

* ✳ A bundle of curiosity whose mark is a curl on top of a dot
* ✳ Shows that a sentence is asking something
* ✳ Used in interrogative sentences: *Who goes there?*

I'm a wily detective. Bent over like my mark, I prod things, pry into them, and demand answers. Who? What? When? Where? Why? How? I'm your partner in every quest for discovery, helping you get to the bottom of any mystery. Who ate the last candy bar? When will Christmas come? Why did the wizard turn the child into a warty toad?

When is a question not a question? Good question! In my years of sleuthing, I've met two kinds of suspects: sneaky indirect questions and up-front direct ones. The indirect guys are phonies. *Jo asked who hit Damian.* That's just a statement in disguise, saying that Jo asked a question and what that question was. Think you can fool me that easily? The direct dudes are the ones I go with. *Who hit Damian?* Now, that's what I call a real question—it needs an answer.

✓ **DO** use a question mark at the end of a direct question. Do use one at the end of a question tag, such as *It costs five dollars, doesn't it?*

✗ **DON'T** use a question mark at the end of an indirect question: *I asked how much it cost.* This is because an indirect question doesn't need an answer.

Question Mark

! Exclamation Point

The Basic Bunch

* Wow! This is the mark with oomph! No kidding!
* It ends a sentence that expresses forceful emotion
* Used after short exclamations, such as *Not again!* or *Ouch!*

Straight up and down, I'm the party-hearty punctuation mark. When things are loud and lively, I'm bound to show up. I've never been shy—some even call me brash. I'm there when you need to be forceful. Imagine if the police used wimpy Question Mark when arresting someone— *Hands up?* instead of *Hands up!* I've got the authority of Period but with an extra knockout punch.

I'm there when you're astonished (*He said that!*), delighted (*You're the best!*), or upset (*Oh no! I can't believe it!*). I bark out commands—*On your mark! Get set! Go!* Watch out, though! Some people overuse me like this!! They think that just putting me at the end of a sentence will add excitement. It won't! I refuse to work in a sentence that doesn't deserve me. I've got my pride.

✓ **DO** use an exclamation point after an expression of strong emotion or a forceful command. Do use one after a word that imitates a sound, such as *Ow!* or *Shh!*

✗ **DON'T** use an exclamation point to get attention for something that isn't truly forceful. Don't use more than one exclamation point at a time.

Exclamation Point

Chapter 2
Up in the Air

"Listen up! We're the Up in the Air crew—punctuation's highfliers." Well, that's what this gang shouts. Think of them as the guys that hover at the shoulders of letters, heads above any of the other punctuation marks. To meet them all, go back to the first sentence on this page— they sit airborne, at the same height as the dots of the "i"s. See, their symbols are like wiggly tadpoles. You need Contraction Apostrophe to help make your sentences sound chatty, Possessive Apostrophe to show who owns what, and those quotation twins to hold a conversation.

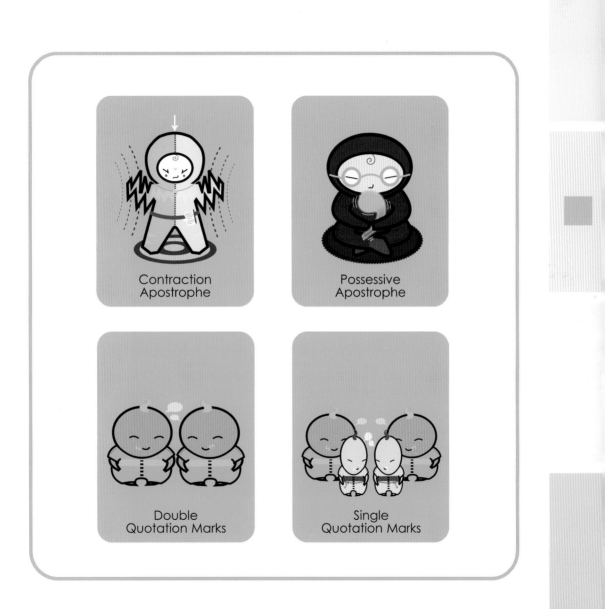

Contraction
Apostrophe

Possessive
Apostrophe

Double
Quotation Marks

Single
Quotation Marks

, **Contraction Apostrophe**

■ Up in the Air

✳ A fussbudget who tells you that something has been left out
✳ Used in place of missing letters—*I'll* instead of "I will"
✳ These shortened forms of two words are called contractions

I'm the kind of person who lends you something and then makes a careful note of what I've lent you and when you're going to give it back. Am I too fussy? Certainly not! I just know when something is missing, and I warn you that it is missing. Take *I've*. What is that in full? "I have." But of course you don't (do not) usually say that. When you're (you are) speaking, you slide over the "ha" in "have" and shrink (contract) the two words into one—*I've*. Fine by me! I'll let you write it the way you say it, but I'll also make sure people know what's being left out—that "ha." Without me, how'd (how would) you know the difference between *she'll* ("she will") and one of those things you find on a beach—a shell?

✓ **DO** use an apostrophe where letters have been left out. Tricky contractions include *can't* for "cannot" and *won't* for "will not."

✗ **DON'T** put the apostrophe in the wrong place. It's *don't*, never *do'nt* (the missing letter is the "o" in "not").

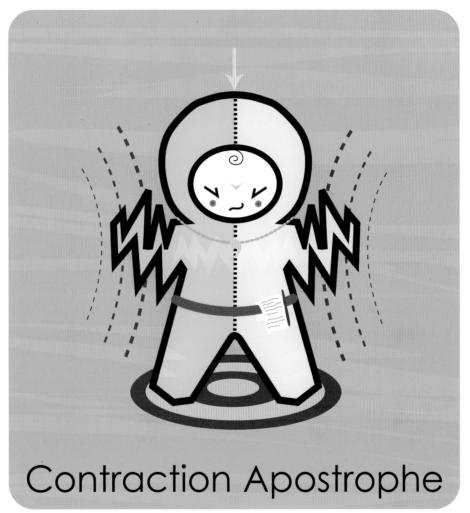

Contraction Apostrophe

, **Possessive Apostrophe**

■ Up in the Air

✹ This neatnik tells you who owns what
✹ In the singular, uses the "–'s" form: *Daisy's hamster*
✹ The plural usually uses the "–s'" form: *The kids' shirts*

When I get ahold of something, that's that—you don't get rid of me. I'm about who owns what, like the nametapes people sew onto their clothes. I'm good to have around if anyone tries to steal something. Hey, that's Ellen's water pistol, not Simon's. *Ellen's, Simon's*—see how I work? I dangle there after the name of the person who owns the thing. If there's just one owner, there's me, then an "s": *the man's hat*. That's true even if a name ends in "s": *Charles's red socks*. I'm more tricky in the plural (if there's more than one owner). If the plural already ends in "s," you use me without the extra "s" at the end: *the kids' chocolate doughnuts*. If it doesn't end in "s," you do add the extra "s": *the children's doughnuts*. Got it?

✓ **DO** use the form "–'s" with singular possessives and plurals not ending in "s." Use the form "–'" (no "s" at the end) with plurals already ending in "s."

✗ **DON'T** use an apostrophe with possessive pronouns: *yours, his, hers, its, ours, theirs.* Don't confuse *its* (belonging to it) with *it's* (a contraction for "it is" or "it has").

Possessive Apostrophe

“ Double Quotation Marks

■ Up in the Air

* Talkative pair, always up for a conversation
* Used for direct speech (the words people actually said)
* They open (") and close (") a quotation

We're the chatterbox twins. Like reflections of each other in a mirror, we stand at the beginning and the end of something that someone said. Like this: *"You're a big ugly fishface."* Sorry about that, but it's what Mary yelled at her brother the other day.

We show that the words between us are the words a person used—not very nice ones in Mary's case. We'll keep the chat going as long as people keep talking, or arguing in the case of Mary and her brother. *He glared at her and muttered, "No, I'm not a fishface. You are." "How dare you say that, you little brat!" she blurted out.* And so they bicker on and on.

✓ **DO** remember that double quotation marks always work in pairs. They show where a quotation begins and where it ends.

✗ **DON'T** forget that in direct speech, when the words quoted form a complete statement, the first word starts with a capital letter: *Abi said, "That's the best cake I've ever tasted."*

Double
Quotation Marks

‘ Single Quotation Marks

■ Up in the Air

✳ Like the chatterbox twins, but less chatty
✳ These pert puppies help you keep the thread of conversations
✳ Without them, you'd soon lose track of who said what to whom

Slim and slender, there's nothing to us at all, but we're the keys to hidden conversational treasures . . . Who doesn't want to hear a bit of gossip—a bit of he-said-she-said? With us you can! Our two pert selves tuck away inside Double Quotation Marks, letting conversations nestle one inside the other. *When I flunked second grade, my father shook his head and said,* "Your grandma said to me, 'Someday you'll have your own kids, and then you'll know why I've got this gray hair.' But she was wrong. Thanks to you, I'm bald, wrinkled, and bananas!" Just what is dear old dad talking about? Dad is reporting the words of his worrywart mother, so his words get Double Quotation Marks and gloomy grandma's grouching gets Single Quotation Marks.

✓ **DO** use single quotation marks to surround exact words (a quotation) when they are reported inside someone else's exact words.

✓ **DO** close the inner quote with single quotation marks, even if the sentence itself ends with double quotation marks.

Single
Quotation Marks

Chapter 3
The Comma Crew

"Commas for clarity!" That's the slogan of the Comma Crew. These tadpole-shaped squiggles on the page have one mission in life—to make things easier to understand inside a sentence. They pack a whole lot of punch. Okay, so they all look the same, but get to know them better and you'll find that each member of the crew has its own special job to do. When a sentence gets longer, these guys ride to your rescue, each taking up its correct position. With them in place, breaking things into chunks, your sentence makes sense and is easy to read.

List-Making
Comma

Joining
Comma

Clause
Comma

Comma
Twins

Comma
Cops

Introducing
Comma

Chatroom Comma

Numbers
Comma

List-Making Comma

The Comma Crew

- ☀ The lineup kid who creates order out of chaos
- ☀ Used to separate the different things in lists, lists, and more lists
- ☀ Listed items can be actions: *He came, ate, and left.*

Break it up! Break it up! I'm the ref who steps in and brings order. What's this jumble of words here? Your big brother has sent you to the store to buy ice cream butter toffee and lollipops—what's that supposed to mean? Is this what you have to buy: ice, cream, butter, toffee, and lollipops—in other words, some ice and some cream and some butter . . . and so on? Or this: ice cream, butter toffee, and lollipops—in other words, some ice cream and some butter toffee and some lollipops?

See what a difference I make! It's the difference between buying the right stuff when you go to the store and getting it all wrong. With me around, placing my commas with due care and attention, you'll never have that kind of mix-up and mayhem.

✓ **DO** use commas to separate words and groups of words when they form a list: *My favorite ice-cream flavors are vanilla, rocky road, and raspberry ripple.*

✗ **DON'T** forget the comma before "and" or "or" in a list with more than two items: *For our vacation, we are going to California, Mexico, or Jamaica.*

List-Making Comma

Joining Comma
The Comma Crew

* Stands at the intersection between two clauses (groups of words)
* Shows where the first clause (mini sentence) ends
* Used with joining words, such as "and," "but," "or," and "yet"

I'm a comma who hangs out at the crossroads, but I'm no villain. Relax! Take it easy! I'm no roadblock. I'm simply here because some sentences are, in fact, two mini sentences (or two clauses) bundled together. They need a joining word (called a conjunction) to link them, and I'm tied in with that.

Look back at our first sentence in the above paragraph. Can you spot its two mini sentences? "I'm a comma who hangs out at the crossroads" and "I'm no villain." What's the joining word? It's "but." And what do you see before "but"? Why me, standing firm at the crossroads. Yes, you'll meet me at the conjunction, a rock-steady sort of guy, making sure that you pause at the right time when you read a sentence. That way, its meaning stays clear.

✓ **DO** use a comma before a conjunction linking two complete clauses: *The prince drew his sword, and the goblins ran away.*

✗ **DON'T** use a comma when the subject of two clauses is the same: *The prince drew his sword and ran toward the goblins.* ("The prince" is the subject in both clauses).

Joining Comma

Clause Comma

The Comma Crew

- ☀ A hingelike comma found at the heart of many sentences
- ☀ Used in sentences with main and subordinate clauses
- ☀ Seen following clauses that begin with "when" and "because"

When the elephant sat at one end of the seesaw, the poor little mouse at the other end went flying into the air. Okay, hold that seesaw in your mind because I'm the pivot—the thing in the middle that the seesaw swings on. I'm like Joining Comma, but different. My sentences have two mini sentences (or two clauses), but here in my kingdom one of the clauses—a snooty so-and-so called the main clause—is more important than the other.

Look back at the first sentence above. The main clause is the one about the mouse—if you think about it, what's interesting is the thought of the mouse flying into the air. The other mini sentence—about the elephant—is the slightly less important part (called the subordinate clause). I'm what marks the turning point between the two.

✓ **DO** use a comma if a subordinate clause (starting with words such as "when" and "after") comes before the main clause: *After I'd eaten my supper, I fell asleep.*

✗ **DON'T** use a comma if a sentence's less important (subordinate) part comes after the main part: *I fell asleep after I'd eaten my supper.*

Clause Comma

, Comma Twins

The Comma Crew

* A trusty twosome who always stick together
* Placed on either side of an interruption in a sentence
* Set off words that aren't vital to a sentence's meaning

Nobody, but nobody, tells us not to interrupt! With us around, you can interrupt yourself, too, right in the middle of a sentence. We, the Comma Twins, slither in and wrap our slinky selves around any word or phrase that barges into a sentence's main point. Read back now and take a peek at us, lolling there on either side of "but nobody," "too," and "the Comma Twins." You don't absolutely need any of those words, do you? But they add a nice little something. When we are around, setting off any interruptions from the rest of the sentence, everything's clear.

Never forget that we are a double act, always traveling as a pair. We refuse to be parted. Keep that in mind and you will find us loyal allies. We are masters of the handy art of wandering off the main point and still making sense.

✓ **DO** use pairs of commas to set off anything nonessential that interrupts a Sentence's main point: *Jake, my best friend, won the race.*

✗ **DON'T** forget to use both of the commas—unless the nonessential word or phrase comes at the end of a sentence: *I won a race, too.* Or *Thanks for your help, Andrew.*

Comma Twins

Comma Cops
The Comma Crew

- Like Comma Twins but more heavy-duty
- Used on either side of mini sentences (clauses) inside sentences
- Often spotted with the words "which" and "who"

We're the Comma Crew's Comma Cops. We check out any clause that thinks it can speed down the middle of a sentence without us. Get a load of this: *The ballet slippers, which had diamond sparkles, were too small for me.* Ha! Did you spot the sneaky clause? Think of it as two ideas dancing around: "The ballet slippers were too small for me" and "The ballet slippers had diamond sparkles." The main clause is about the ballet slippers being too small. The diamond clause slots inside the main clause for a little extra . . . well, sparkle.

Always on the alert, we roar in and place a comma, like a traffic cone, at each end of the extra clause. Just doing our duty! We love a bit of bling, but we've got to keep the fast lane clear for the sentence's main idea.

✓ **DO** use pairs of commas to set off clauses that aren't essential to the sentence's main point: *Susie, who loves candy, felt sick.*

✗ **DON'T** set off clauses that say something essential to the sentence's main point: *The dog that bit him was brown* ("that bit him" is essential information).

Comma Cops

Introducing Comma

The Comma Crew

- ☀ Part of a warm-up act before a sentence really gets going
- ☀ Used after introductory words at the start of some sentences
- ☀ Also comes after a name, as in *Sammy, go home!*

Greetings, I'm your host for this evening's show, here to present a dazzling cast of stars. You see, the star part in any sentence—the part that says the really important things—sometimes likes an introduction, a word or two to go at the beginning. Well, that's where I fit in. Yes, I'm the member of the Comma Crew that shows where the intro ends and the main part of the sentence begins.

Of course, the few words at the start aren't totally necessary. Lop off "Greetings," "You see," "Well," "Yes," and "Of course" from the sentences above and they still make sense. But hey, you know what stars are like. They just love to be talked about. By the way, although stars love the intros, they hate it if the intros butt in and steal the show. That's why I stand between them.

✓ **DO** use a single comma after a word or phrase that introduces a sentence's main clause: *For me, blueberries are the best fruit.*

✗ **DON'T** use a comma after an "-ing" phrase at the start of a sentence if the phrase is the subject of the sentence: *Eating ice cream is fun.*

Introducing Comma

Chatroom Comma

The Comma Crew

* One half of the gossiping duo Comma and Quotation Mark
* Introduces direct speech (the words people actually said)
* Found with words such as "said," "asked," and "replied"

Watch what you say—we've got you bugged. Years ago, I got the job of introducing quotations, and I've been doing it ever since. When you see me looming in a sentence before Double Quotation Mark, chances are some dirt is gonna be dished. Like this: *Tom said, "We're raiding the refrigerator at midnight." Hannah replied, "Okay, dude, I'll be there." Then Sharon asked, "Who's going to keep the dog quiet?"* (Certain people were very interested when we reported that to them.)

See how I operate? I'm the comma that comes at the end of the intro and before the thing the person said. Sometimes I step into the middle of a quotation. It's done in pairs, like this: *"That's fine," said Andy, "but I've got a problem. I'm hungry now. I can't wait till midnight."*

✓ **DO** use a comma between the introduction to a quotation and the quotation itself: *She said to him, "You're the stupidest person in the whole world."*

✗ **DON'T** use a comma if the quotation is short and not a complete sentence: *She called him "the stupidest person in the whole world."*

Chatroom Comma

Numbers Comma

The Comma Crew

- ☀ This orderly fella is best known in thousands—or 1,000s
- ☀ Makes it much easier to read large numbers
- ☀ Can also separate the different parts of a date

Hey, hey, slow down! Take it easy, take it step by step—that's my motto. What are these numbers you're rattling off? Somebody told you that there are 37308 gumdrops in the average candy store? Well, I'll take your word for it, but what a jumble of figures! Let's sort it out. There are 37,308 gumdrops—or thirty-seven thousand (the part before my comma) three hundred eight (after my comma) gumdrops. Presto! When you move from hundreds to thousands, there I am, and everything's clearer.

Remember Comma Crew's slogan: "Commas for clarity!" That applies to dates, too. When was your little sister born? *Tuesday September 12 2006*. No, no, that's not the way. Remember, step by step. *My little sister, Joy, was born on Tuesday, September 12, 2006*. Nice and clear!

✓ **DO** use commas in large numbers to set off thousands, millions, billions, trillions, and so on: 1,000; 1,000,000; 1,000,000,000; 1,000,000,000,000.

✗ **DON'T** put commas in year dates. The American Revolution began in the year 1776, not 1,776.

Numbers Comma

Chapter 4
Divide and Conquer

Chapter Four. Level Four! See, you're about to meet six of the most feared marks in the punctuation mix. Use these ingredients correctly and you'll add a rich, delicate flavor; use them incorrectly and you'll make a mud pie of a sentence—yuck! Although the Divide and Conquer gang love to boast among themselves about their tasty zing, they hate to be misused or overused. Like everything else in the punctuation kingdom, their rules are simple and their job is to help with the flow. You won't get kudos for plunking in these marks willy-nilly—just confusion.

Parentheses

Dash

Hyphen

Ellipsis

Colon

Semicolon

( ) **Parentheses**

Divide and Conquer

* Rounded brackets that always come in pairs
* Mainly used to fence off interruptions from the main sentence
* Seen hugging explanations and additional information

We are twins, full of gossip, juicy details, and small comments on things. The main sentence plods along, giving all the important (but, to be perfectly honest, often pretty boring) stuff. Then we burst in, making things more lively with our own special take on the subject. And here's the good news: it's okay to butt in—not rude at all. As long as you begin and end an interruption with one of us (just keep the interruption fairly short), it's allowed. Hooray!

That old stick-in-the-mud Sentence knows that it will still make sense (and be shorter) without what's inside us. Strictly speaking, he's right. But don't think we're just flibbertigibbets, filling the air with our silly chatter. We often give key information (such as an explanation or a date) that helps Sentence make his point.

✓ **DO** use parentheses for nonessential information (such as a date) that explains, adds to, or comments on the meaning of the main sentence.

✗ **DON'T** use just one parenthesis—you need two (one at each end). Don't make the interruption so long that a reader loses track of what the sentence is saying.

()

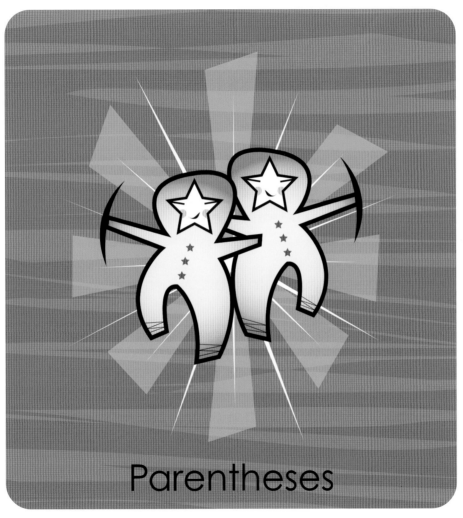

Parentheses

— **Dash**

▥ Divide and Conquer

- ✳ Extra-long horizontal line that is nothing like Hyphen
- ✳ Alerts you to an interruption in a sentence—like a speed bump
- ✳ Can go in place of "from/to": *1939–1945*

Wow! It's so thrilling. You'll never guess what the kids found lying fast asleep in the apple tree—a baby dragon! That's me when I'm used on my own—a pause followed by a giant twist or leap. This wonderful effect is what makes me different from that stuffy Colon. With Colon, you can be sure that there's no suspense: what follows is pretty much what you'd expect. With me, who knows where you'll end up—maybe with a baby dragon.

Often I'm all alone, but I can also come as one of an identical pair. When that happens, my twin and I are usually doing the same job as Parentheses but in a more laid-back way. Parentheses can be a little too much—like fans mobbing a movie star—while we smile sweetly and wave as you go by.

✓ **DO** use a dash for a sudden break or interruption in a sentence. Do use a pair of dashes if the interruption is in the middle of the sentence.

✗ **DON'T** use a pair of dashes if the interruption comes at the end of the sentence. Don't use a single dash and a pair of dashes in the same sentence.

Dash

– Hyphen
▥ Divide and Conquer

✺ A tiny-but-mighty punctuation mark that's in and out of fashion
✺ Used to connect words, not break up sentences
✺ Its job is to make words clear: *re-sent* isn't *resent*

I'm the awe-inspiring Hyphen! A short flick of your pen and you've commanded two words to act as one—a real high-wire act! I neatly notch together descriptive words before nouns to create brand-new expressions called compound adjectives. So, is the class bully a *mean kid* or a *mean-as-a-snake kid*?

I'm also used to form compound words, such as *do-gooder* or *dog-sitter*. I'm often thrown away, though, when a hyphenated word becomes familiar: the 1960s' *mini-skirt* is today's *miniskirt*. You should always use me with the prefixes "ex-," "self-," and "all-." But it's usually clearer if I'm not there after other prefixes, such as "anti," "co," and "pre." Hyphenated last names use me, too: *Powell-Hartzell, Rex-Snodsworth*!

✓ **DO** use in compound adjectives: *pretty-as-a-pearl girl*. Do use in compound words: *go-cart, one-way*. Do use with some prefixes: *ex-wife, self-employed, all-inclusive*.

✗ **DON'T** use a hyphen to link descriptive words if one of the words is an adverb ending in "ly": *neatly combed hair* (NOT *neatly-combed hair*).

Hyphen

... **Ellipsis**

▥ Divide and Conquer

✸ Row of three dots that needs to be used with caution
✸ Used to show words missing or left out of whole quotations
✸ Sleepy character who is famous for his timely snoozes

Yeah, well . . . some people find me kind of . . . well, you know . . . quite annoying, actually . . . 'cause I, like . . . leave words out of sentences and sort of drift off . . . But, really, that's so unfair, you know . . . because that's my job.

Strictly speaking, you should use my dots only in direct quotations (the exact thing that was said or written). Let's say your whole quotation is as follows: "Friends, Romans, countrymen, lend me your ears"—that's Shakespeare—and you want to leave out the "Romans, countrymen" stuff. Well, use me: *"Friends . . . lend me your ears."* (Ever lent a friend your ears? It's painful, man.) But, actually, in real life, you can use me in other ways . . . like if you want to leave people guessing a bit . . . like you've told them enough and they can just figure out the rest . . .

✓ **DO** use an ellipsis to show that you've left some words out of a direct quotation or that a thought has been left incomplete.

✗ **DON'T** overuse ellipses. Don't use an ellipsis just because you've run out of ideas on a subject.

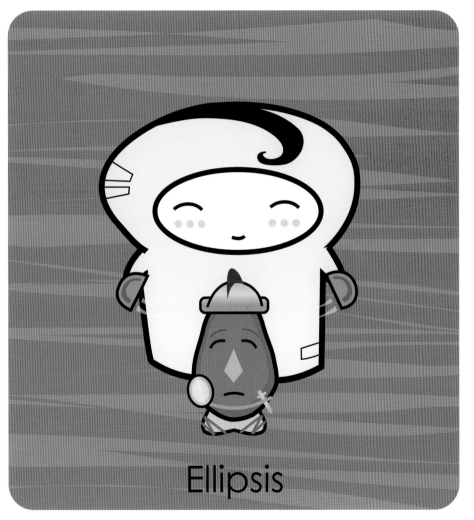

Ellipsis

: Colon

Divide and Conquer

- ☀ Pair of dots that introduces things: it often means "that is to say"
- ☀ Used to mark a clear break in a sentence before an explanation
- ☀ Seen before quotations: "Too many cooks spoil the broth."

Beep! Beep! It's 7:15, time to get up! Can you spot me? I'm the mark used to separate hours from minutes. But that's a duty and not my main job. I'm a pretty powerful punctuation mark. See, there's one thing I hate more than anything else: confusion! I have logic to the way I work: the intro comes first, then me, followed by extra explanations or nitty-gritty details.

I like things to be orderly. One of my favorite places to stand is in front of lists: lists of the ingredients to make a magic potion, lists of your ten best friends and five deadliest enemies, lists of top-scoring sports stars, and any other list you can think of. You won't use me that often, but when you use me properly, you can be certain of one thing: I'll give clout to what you write.

✓ **DO** use a colon to explain or add extra details to the part of the sentence before the colon or to introduce a list. Do use to separate hours from minutes.

✗ **DON'T** put a space before a colon, and never follow it with a dash or a hyphen.

54

Colon

; Semicolon

▥ Divide and Conquer

☀ This character's motto is "Fair's fair"
☀ Used to join two whole sentences that are closely connected
☀ Takes the place of List-Making Comma in long, troublesome lists

I'm a wizard at showing that there are two sides to a thing. On one hand, the Harry Potter stories are very exciting; on the other hand, the Narnia stories are less grisly. If you think about it, that last sentence is really two sentences, but what they talk about is so closely linked that it seems silly to put Period between them. So use my wizard's wand and, presto, the two become one. My magic works best when the two mini sentences are of equal importance: *Wizards use wands; witches prefer spells.*

I'm also useful for lists that have gotten too complicated for List-Making Comma: *I bought some antiwerewolf potion to give to Tabitha; a simple spell kit and supplies for Linus; five wands made from holly wood; a new blue wizard's hat and cloak; and a superslick new broomstick.*

✓ **DO** use a semicolon when two sentences are so closely related that a period would be too strong. Do use semicolons for complicated lists.

✗ **DON'T** use a semicolon with "and" or "but" (except in a list). For example: *Dipak likes football, but Kevin prefers hockey. Or Dipak likes football; Kevin prefers hockey.*

Semicolon

Basic Grammar

Words are divided into eight different groups, called the parts of speech.

Nouns Words used to name things, such as people, places, and objects.

Pronouns Words used in the place of a noun, such as *he*, *her*, *them, my*, and *their*.

Verbs Words that tell you what someone or something is doing or being, such as *sit* or *eat*.

Adjectives Words that describe or tell you more about a noun, such as *wet* (as in *a wet cloth*).

Adverbs Words that describe or tell you more about a verb, such as *slowly* (as in *she walked slowly*). Adverbs can also describe adjectives and other adverbs.

Prepositions Words that tell you how one thing relates to another, such as *under* (as in *the road under the bridge*).

Conjunctions Words that join other words or groups of words, such as *and*, *but*, and *or*.

Interjections Words that express strong feelings, such as *wow*, *gosh*, and *yuck*.

SPOT THE PARTS OF SPEECH

The kid gobbled a hamburger.
1. This sentence has two nouns and a verb. Have you spotted them? (See below for the answers.)

The hungry kid greedily gobbled a huge hamburger.
2. The sentence now has two adjectives and an adverb. What are they?

The hungry kid greedily gobbled a huge hamburger, and he still wanted a gooey dessert.
3. It's getting more complicated. Have you spotted the conjunction and the pronoun? What are they?
4. The sentence now has two clauses—two mini sentences for the price of one. What are they?

Answers
1. Nouns: "kid," "hamburger." Verb: "gobbled."
2. Adjectives: "hungry" (describing the kid), "huge" (describing the hamburger). Adverb: "greedily" (describing how the kid gobbled the hamburger).
3. Conjunction: "and" (joining the two halves of the sentence).
Pronoun: "he" (used in place of "the kid").
4. First clause: "The hungry . . . huge hamburger." Second clause: "and he still wanted a gooey dessert."

Index

Glossary

Abbreviation A shortened form of a word—for example: *Dr.* for "Doctor," or *Sept.* for "September."

Active voice A sentence where the subject of the sentence performs the action—the opposite of passive voice. In *The dog ate the cookies*, "dog" (the subject) performs the action, "ate."

Clause A group of words that has a subject and a predicate. There are two types: a main clause makes complete sense on its own; a subordinate clause makes sense only with the main clause. In *Sandra drank some lemonade because she was thirsty*, "Sandra drank some lemonade" is the main clause, and "because she was thirsty" is the subordinate clause.

Complex sentence A sentence made up of a main clause and a subordinate clause.

Compound sentence A sentence made up of two simple sentences, joined by a comma, a colon, a semicolon, or a connecting word.

Consonant Any letter in the alphabet that is not a vowel.

Contraction A shortening of two words into one, using Contraction Apostrophe—for example: *I'm* for "I am."

Direct question A straightforward question—for example: *Where did you go on vacation?*

Direct speech The exact words a person speaks.

Emphasis The amount of emotion when you speak—for example: *Get up, Fred!* is strong emphasis; *It's time* *to get up, Fred* is normal emphasis.

Exclamation A word or sentence used to express a strong feeling or emotion.

Indirect question A question in the grammatical form of a statement—for example: *My mother asked where you went on vacation.*

Interrogative sentence A sentence in the form of a question—for example: *Are you rich or poor?*

Object The person or thing affected by the verb in a sentence. In *Oliver kicked the ball*, "ball" is the object.

Paragraph A group of sentences that talk about a single topic. They are marked with an indentation in the first line or an extra space between lines.

Passive voice A sentence where the subject of the sentence has an action done to it—the opposite of active voice. In *The cookies were eaten by the dog*, "cookies" (the subject) have an action done to them.

Phrase A group of words without a verb and that is not a sentence—for example: *A toothy grin*.

Plural More than one of a person or thing—the opposite of singular: *oranges* and *beaches* are examples of plural nouns.

Predicate The words written or said about the subject— a predicate always contains a verb. In *Susan ate a slice of lemon meringue pie*, "Susan" is the subject and "ate a slice of lemon meringue pie" is the predicate.

Glossary

Punctuation marks The traffic signals of the writing world. Without them, your writing would be nothing but a jumble of letters!

Silent letters Letters that are not pronounced but that are written in the correct spelling of a word—for example: the "k" in *knight*.

Simple sentence A sentence with only one subject and one predicate.

Singular One person or thing: *orange* and *beach* are examples of singular nouns.

Subject The person or thing doing the action in the sentence. In *Oliver kicked the ball*, "Oliver" is the thing doing the action. All sentences have a subject and a predicate.

Suffix A set of letters added to the end of a word—for example: "able" to "comfort" to form *comfortable*.

Syllable An uninterrupted sound formed from a set of one or more vowels and one or more consonants. The word "syllable" has three syllables: *syl-la-ble*.

Tense The form of a verb that shows when an action takes place. The main tenses are past, present, and future—for example, *drank*, *drink*, and *will drink*.

Vowel Any letter in the alphabet that is not a consonant: *a, e, i, o, u*, and sometimes *y*.